The Life and Times of Saint Patrick
Wyatt North

Wyatt North Publishing

About Wyatt North Publishing

Wyatt North Publishing is a boutique publishing company. We always provide high quality, perfectly formatted, Books.

We guarantee our Books. If you are not 100% satisfied we will do everything in our power to make you happy. Visit WyattNorth.com for more information. Please feel free to contact us with any questions or comments. We welcome your feedback by email at info@WyattNorth.com.

Foreword

One part biography, one part prayer book, The Life and Prayers of Saint Patrick is an essential for any Christian.

The Saint Patrick of his own writings and the early records of his life are not known to many. While Saint Patrick also represents shamrocks, Irish pride, and even the occasional green beer there is much of his life that is often forgotten. For instance, the original color associated with Saint Patrick's Day was blue, and although Saint Patrick dedicated his life to spreading Christianity in Ireland, he might not have celebrated the nation, as we do on his feast day today, in his own lifetime. Ireland, for Patrick, was in many ways bittersweet.

On the other hand, it was also the nation of his spiritual awakening, which is probably a large part of why Patrick decided to make the conversion of Ireland his calling. In the English-speaking world, few saints are as well known, yet so misunderstood, as Saint Patrick. The saint himself, as he was in life, sometimes gets lost in his holiday. The seekers who want to know the real Patrick have to dig much deeper, but they will also find Patrick a more complex and rewarding acquaintance.

Enjoy.

About Wyatt North Publishing..3

Foreword 4

Quick Facts..6

The Life of Saint Patrick 8

    Introduction 9

    The Birth of Saint Patrick..14

    Patrick's Youth...21

    The Lord's Blessing..27

    A Missionary's Education...34

    First Irish Mission 40

    Second Irish Mission 51

Prayers of Saint Patrick 60

    Prayers for the Faithful..61

    Prayer for God's Protection and Christ's Presence....................63

    Lorica of Saint Patrick 65

Quick Facts

The new "Quick Facts" section in **The Life and Prayers** collection provides the reader with a collection of facts about each saint!

Born:

Between 387 and 390

Died:

Likely between 461 and 464 at Saul, County Down, Ireland of natural causes

Feast:

March 17

Attributes:

Cross, serpent, shamrock

The Life of Saint Patrick

Introduction

I, *Patrick, a sinner and unlearned, have been appointed bishop in*

Ireland, and I accept from
God what I am. I dwell amongst the barbarians as a proselyte and
a fugitive for the love of God.

So Saint Patrick describes himself, in the opening of his Epistle to Coroticus. He goes on to address his readers with kinship as "[his] own people," but Saint Patrick is not speaking to the Irish — he is addressing the British.

The Saint Patrick of his own writings and the early records of his life are not known to many. While Saint Patrick also represents shamrocks, Irish pride, and even the occasional green beer there is much of his life that is often forgotten. For instance, the original color associated with Saint Patrick's Day was blue, and although Saint Patrick dedicated his life to spreading Christianity in Ireland, he might not have celebrated the nation, as we do on his feast day today, in his own lifetime. Ireland, for Patrick, was in many ways bittersweet.

On the other hand, it was also the nation of his spiritual awakening, which is probably a large part of why Patrick decided to make the conversion of Ireland his calling. In the

English-speaking world, few saints are as well known, yet so misunderstood, as Saint Patrick. The saint himself, as he was in life, sometimes gets lost in his holiday. The seekers who want to know the real Patrick have to dig much deeper, but they will also find Patrick a more complex and rewarding acquaintance.

As we set out on a quest for the real Saint Patrick we begin, of course, with the words from his own pen.

Only two writings of Patrick's remain. The earliest is probably his Epistle to Coroticus, a letter that Patrick wrote to the subjects of the British Christian chieftain Coroticus, so that they may persuade him to release the Christians his allied soldiers had captured and enslaved from one of Patrick's communities. It was written sometime in the 5th century, towards the end of Patrick's earthly life. The second text of Saint Patrick's that comes down to us is his Confessions. Unlike Saint Augustine of Hippo's Confessions, which were probably his source of inspiration, Saint Patrick's Confessions are not declarations of past sinfulness. Rather, they are declarations of the ways in which God has favored Patrick and worked through him, throughout Patrick's life. Although it is not an autobiography, it contains several autobiographic passages in which Patrick gives us his own view of his life.

Saint Patrick is also mentioned in a text that is contemporary to himself, but written by someone else: Saint Sechnall's <u>Hymn of Saint Patrick</u>. Saint Sechnall was personally close to Patrick and worked with him in Ireland. He was also Patrick's nephew. The text itself, however, can be rather frustrating for the seeker of Patrick as, although it paints a beautiful picture of the saint, it contains very little in terms of biographical material.

The earliest life of Saint Patrick may have been written in the 6th century. It was written on verse, entirely in Irish, and is known as the <u>Metrical Life of St. Patrick</u>. It is said to have been written by Saint Fiacc, one of Saint Patrick's earliest converts in Ireland. Unfortunately, it has always been popular to attribute anonymous texts to much earlier personages, so the text may in fact be as much as a century or two younger. That would make the earliest hagiographies of Saint Patrick two Latin texts written around the 660s or 670s, two hundred years after the death of Saint Patrick. They are both called <u>Vita sancti Patricii</u> and were written by Tírechán and Muirchu moccu Machtheni respectively. Both authors used a now lost 7th century book called the <u>Book of Ultán</u> as a source. The 9th century life of Saint Patrick, <u>Vita tripartita Sancti Patricii</u>, is the oldest source for many of the more miraculous aspects of Saint Patrick's works. It is a bilingual Latin and Irish text in three parts, each meant to be read on a separate day of a three day festival of Saint Patrick. It has clearly inspired later hagiographers, such as Jocelyn of Furness writing his <u>Life and Acts of Saint Patrick</u> in the late 12th or early 13th century. There are also numerous late legends with similarly miraculous and magical aspects, such as the late 13th century <u>Acallam na Senórach</u>, in which Patrick converses with immortal pagan warriors from Ireland's mythic past.

The Birth of Saint Patrick

Contrary to modern perception, Saint Patrick was not Irish.

Patrick himself writes that he was born in Bannven Taberniae in Roman Britain. Tradition has always placed Patrick's birthplace on the western coast of Britain, near the Irish Sea, so although a Bannven has been discovered near Daventry in eastern England Patrick is probably referring to a different town.

The Metrical Life of Saint Patrick, which may have been written by Saint Fiacc who knew Patrick personally, tells us that Patrick was born in Nemthur, another name that we unfortunately lack a precise geographical understanding for. The only relatively early life of Saint Patrick that specifies a known region is the Vita tripartita Sancti Patricii, which tells us that Patrick's Bannven Taberniae lay the region of Alcluaid, around modern Dumbarton on the western coast of the Scottish lowlands.

Roman Britain around the birth of Saint Patrick was in a pressing state of uncertainty. The Picts, a Pagan people in northern Scotland, were steadily pushing downwards, expanding their territory and raiding Roman fortresses and cities. They were such a strong force that it has traditionally been thought that Roman troops withdrew entirely from Scotland and northern England by 383, before the birth of Saint

Patrick.

This would have left northern Britain very vulnerable to foreign marauders, especially around the Scottish lowlands where Patrick may have been born. Archaeologists have been changing that image slightly, as they have found some Roman coins around the outposts on Hadrian's Wall that date to after 383. This means that there were probably Roman troops at least on some of the larger northern outposts after 383. In addition to the Picts, the Britons were frequently being raided by the Scoti, a Pagan Gaelic people from Ireland who subsequently settled in Scotland and gave it its name.

The pressure was not only coming from the north, it was also coming from the south and the east as more and more Pagan Saxons crossed over from modern Germany. Despite these foreign threats, the Britons saw the Roman legions decrease, as they were withdrawn to protect what emperors considered to be more important borders of the increasingly unsustainable empire. The economy was falling and the military was failing. The times must have been felt quite strongly, especially by the upper classes.

Patrick's father, Calpurnius, belonged to such an upper class. Although he did not belong to the aristocratic class who served as local senators, he was a landowning man in a country where most people rented land or worked land as servants or slaves. This meant that he was forced to act as decurion, a municipal council member, for his region. It was certainly not an enviable title. His duties involved calculating, collecting, and delivering taxes, and should he fail to deliver what was expected of him it might very well come out of his own pocket.

This was in a time when corruption was exceedingly high in the provinces, so chances are that as a decurion your superiors would expect excess taxes to fill their own coffers in addition to those of the emperor. Combined with the great economic decline that must have affected everyone, being decurion was unlikely to make you any friends. In fact, it was such an unenviable position that the Emperor Maxentius used to punish Christians for their perceived religious deviance by promoting them to the status of decurion.

Many preferred to sell their land and lose their status than to do the decurion's work. Another way to get out of a decurion obligation was to seek ordination within the Church, as those ordained could not hold political offices. Because priests were not required to be celibate, ordination did not have to mean a great change for these people. So many turned to the Church in order to get out of their decurion obligations that, around the time that Saint Patrick was born, the emperor Theodosius the Great created a law stating that any decurion who sought ordination would forfeit his lands to the state. Calpurnius was ordained deacon before the law was passed, so his lands remained within the family. His father, Potitus, before him had been ordained a priest to avoid political office, and his brother Odisse was also a deacon.

Patrick's mother's name may have been Conchessa. Patrick himself never tells us her name, but it is given in the <u>Vita tripartita Sancti Patricii</u> and Jocelyn's <u>Life and Acts of Saint Patrick</u>. According to these sources she was either a sister or a niece of Saint Martin of Tours, whose parents had sold her and her sister into servitude under Patrick's father. Calpurnius in turn was so charmed by this beautiful and cultured Roman Gaulish lady that he raised her from the position of lowly serving maid to wife. Most scholars today do not take such claims seriously, as it was once popular to imagine a sacred family tree for beloved saints.

Patrick was born around the year 389. Like many other British Romans at the time, he probably had both a Roman and a British name. His Roman name was Patricius, whence we get the English version: Patrick. He may also have had a Roman surname, traditionally thought to be Magonus, a Latinized version of the

British name Maewyn. According to Saint Fiacc, Patrick's birth name was actually Succat, so it is possible that this was his British name. Perhaps he wore it, like some Romans did, as a cognomen, making his full Roman name Patricius Magonus Sucatus. When speaking to the Britons he may then well have been Maewyn Succat. Of his siblings we only know that he had a sister, whose name is given as Lupait.

It is said in the <u>Vita tripartita Sancti Patricii</u> that Saint Patrick was born on top of a flag stone, and ever since that day the stone would bring forth water any time someone swore a false oath upon it. The same source tells us about the miraculous baptism of Saint Patrick. We are told that when the man St. Patrick was born, he was taken to "a blind, flat-faced man" to be baptized. This priest's name was Gornias. For some reason, they went ahead with the baptism even though they had no water to perform the baptism with. That is to say, they had no water until Gornias made the sign of the cross with the infant Patrick's hand and a fountain of water burst forth from the ground below. The water washed over Gornias's face, and suddenly he could see. But, that was not the greatest miracle of them all: Gornias, who had been blind all of his life and had not learned the alphabet, picked up the book and read the whole baptism himself. Unfortunately, this baptism story contradicts Patrick's own writings, which indicate that he was not baptized until he was at least 15 years old.

Patrick's Youth

Since Patrick was the son of a deacon, the grandson of a priest, and belonged to the upper classes, he most likely received a Christian education. He must have learned to read and write some Latin, and what it meant to be a Christian.

Of Patrick's childhood in general very little is known. Patrick himself says very little about it, except that he grew up in a small country house, and it is only the sources from the 9th century and forward that provide some real childhood narratives. According to these sources, "many prodigies and miracles were wrought by Patrick in his youth."

Those prodigies and miracles often include interaction between Patrick and his beloved nurse. Once, in the wintertime, Patrick was out playing in the snow as children do. When he had finished playing outside, he gathered as much ice as he could carry and he brought it inside to his nurse. His nurse admonished him: "It would be better for you to bring us withered brambles to warm ourselves with than what you have brought." Patrick responded: "Believe thou, because God is powerful thereto that even the sheets of ice will burn like fagots." And so they did.

Another time, we are told, Patrick was standing watch over the sheep and a wild wolf came and carried off one of the lambs. Patrick's nurse was very upset and reproached him for failing to keep proper watch. That next morning the wolf carried the lamb back to the very spot that it was taken, completely unharmed.

A different story involves one of the family cows. According to the Vita tripartita Sancti Patricii the cow simply went mad, but according to the later Life and Acts of Saint Patrick by Jocelyn of Furness the cow was possessed by an evil spirit. In its madness, or possession, the cow killed five other cows. By this time, Patrick's nurse had understood what a special child the blessed Patrick was, so she asked him to resuscitate the dead cows. So he did, and then he healed, or exorcised, the afflicted cow, and all was well.

One of these tales hints at Patrick's relationship with his sister, Lupait. Once when they were out on the farm together, Lupait tripped while running to Patrick, and she struck her head on a stone. Just as her spirit was about to leave her body, Patrick made the sign of the cross over her head and instantly she was healed.

This tradition of Saint Patrick as a holy child fits beautifully into the saintly tradition at the time that these texts were written, and can help us understand the modern image of Saint Patrick and what it means to be a Saint, but they are in direct contradiction to what little Patrick himself says of his childhood.

In his Confessions he tells us that he "had gone away from God, and did not keep his commandments," nor did the child Patrick "listen to [his] priests, who advised [him] about how [he] could be saved." He goes as far as to say: "I did not then believe in the living God, not even when I was a child. In fact, I remained in death and unbelief until I was reproved strongly, and actually brought low by hunger and nakedness daily."

Of course, it could be that Saint Patrick was being humble in writing about himself, but why would he lie and create a past for himself where he was neither baptized nor faithful? Chances are that he must mention it because it was, during his lifetime, widely known that Patrick had been less than a model citizen, and there was a wide-spread opinion that Patrick had not been a qualified candidate to become Bishop of the Irish.

Patrick alludes to this opinion in his Confessions. He tells us that some people had argued that Patrick's ordination was void, because he had committed such sins as would bar him from ordination. The sin was such that some thirty years after the event, it was expected by some to change everything, and it haunted Patrick throughout his entire earthly life, although he had confessed it before God and he himself felt that his subsequent baptism had spiritually cleansed him. Patrick does not tell us which sin it was that he had committed. All that he says is this: "some things I had done one day – rather, in one hour – when I was young, before I overcame my weakness […] I was then fifteen years old."

It was not long after that day, or that hour, before his sixteenth birthday, that Patrick's life changed forever. The event that changed everything was the arrival of marauders from the west. A fleet of Gaelic freebooters fell upon Calpurnius's farmstead, capturing some and probably killing many others. They loaded the prisoners onto a ship and they brought them across the Irish Sea, to be sold into slavery.

He was clearly still a student at the time, or had been pulled out of his schooling for other reasons, having not yet fully mastered the Latin language. Perhaps as a result of this sudden change, he never really did. Patrick himself says of the language: "For me, however, my speech and words have been translated into a foreign language, as it can be easily seen from my writings the standard of the instruction and learning I have had." Patrick also tells us more directly how his time in slavery stunted his more academic development: "I was taken prisoner as a youth, particularly young in the matter of being able to speak, and before I knew what I should seek and what I should avoid. That is why, today, I blush and am afraid to expose my lack of experience, because I can't express myself with the brief words I would like in my heart and soul."

There are contradictory traditions concerning where Patrick ended up once he had been captured. There is a very strong tradition that places Patrick's years of slavery were spent in Ulster, in modern Northern Ireland, under a master by the name of Miliucc, for whom Patrick is supposed to have served as a pig herdsman. In Patrick's own words, however, he spent the entirety of his slave years under a single master in Connaught, in western Ireland near the coast. There he spent six years herding sheep. And it was in those days that Patrick came to know the Lord.

The Lord's Blessing

Patrick wrote of his slavery, "It was there that the Lord

opened up my awareness of my lack of faith. Even though it
came about late, I recognized my failings. So I turned with all my
heart to the Lord my God, and he looked down on my lowliness
and had mercy on my youthful ignorance." We do not know if it
was a change that came upon Patrick immediately after his
capture, or if it was something that developed over time.

The skeptic may say that it would not be the first time that a
casual, or cultural, Christian found the Lord as the result of
suddenly desperately needing him to exist, but even the hardest
skeptic can't deny that in the end it does not matter whether
Patrick opened up his heart to God, or God shone a light into
Patrick's heart. The result is the same, and from Patrick's
subjective experience there is no difference. The Lord entered
Patrick's life, and He entered it with an immense force. In those
days of slavery in Connaught, Patrick felt that the Lord was ever
present, protecting and consoling him "as a father does for his
son."

It was then that Patrick truly began to pray. He prayed
frequently during the day. He would pray more than a hundred
times each day, and then offer nearly as many prayers every

night. He was "roused to prayer, in snow, in ice, and rain" yet he "never felt the worse for it."

So it continued for six years. If Patrick had any moments of doubt, he has not relayed them to us in any of the writing that survives. Rather, he tells us that each day his love for God, and his fear of God, increased, and it intensified his prayers. We don't know how Patrick's master and the other servants may have looked upon the shepherd's frequent and fervent prayer.

It is quite possible that there were other Christians, whether from Britain, France or Ireland, serving under Patrick's master, who helped each other keep faith strong, but, if there were, Patrick does not mention them in his writings. If there was such a group, it could probably operate quite openly, and if there was not one then Patrick could probably still be quite openly Christian. It was generally more troublesome for a Christian to serve under a Pagan master, than it was for a Pagan to have Christian servants. This was simply because the Pagan master had a world-view that supported multiple powerful and beneficent deities, one of which was the Christian God, whereas the Christian servant had an understanding that the master was worshiping evil demonic forces, which indirectly placed them under the thumb of the devil.

One night, six years into slavery, Patrick had a dream. In this dream a voice came to him and told him: "You do well to fast. Fasting, you shall soon return to your native land." Waking up, Patrick continued to offer hundreds of prayer each day, but he also began to fast like the voice had told him.

Just a few nights later, the voice came to him again in another dream. "Behold," it said, "your ship is ready," and in his dream Patrick could see the place where his ship was waiting for him. It was far away in the northeast of the island, in a region where Patrick had never been and did not know anyone. When Patrick woke up, he ran; and, though he was a fugitive slave, crossing unknown mountains and forests with countless dangers, Patrick tells us that he was not afraid. He knew in his heart that God was guiding him.

The ship that Patrick ended up finding was a trading ship, carrying highly valued Irish hunting dogs to Roman clients in southern Europe. In order to secure a place on the ship, Patrick offered to work for his passage, but while the crew was initially positive to taking him on board he was turned down.

Patrick did not give up easily. As he turned away to find a more quiet place to pray, he heard the voice of one of the ship's crew members calling out to him: "Come quickly, for they are calling for you!" The captain had changed his mind. Patrick would be allowed to work for his passage on the ship after all.

Patrick provides nearly no details concerning the crew's itinerary. We learn that they traveled by sea for three days, and because Patrick says nothing more of that journey we tend to assume that it was an uneventful trip and that the ship made average time. Having disembarked on mainland, Patrick, the crew, and the living cargo, traveled another 25 days by foot in the wilderness before meeting a single person.

This tells us that the ship cannot have taken Patrick directly to his "native land," as one might assume based on Patrick's first dream. There is no place in Britain that is three days at sea from Ireland and is sufficiently wild and abandoned that one could walk for more than three weeks before finding a settlement. The most likely landing port would be in the southern half of western France, perhaps near modern Bordeaux. By the early 5th century, there were large deserted and wild landmasses in southern France. Since Patrick is recorded having frequently spoken to his disciples about his otherwise unrecorded journeys through France and Italy, it seems likely that the large landmass crossed was the south of France and the north of Italy.

After several weeks of walking in the wilderness, supplies were running low. Men and dogs were both in danger of starving to death, and nothing seemed to help. Perhaps irritation from hunger and exhaustion provided some dissonance between the Pagan crew and the Christian

Patrick, for the captain said to him: "Now, Christian, you say that your God is great and almighty. Why then don't you pray for us? For we are in danger of starvation and there is little chance we will come upon help."

Patrick replied: "Nothing is impossible to the Lord, my God. Turn to him honestly, that he may send you food in your path this day until you are filled, for God has plenty in all places."

Soon afterwards, a herd of pigs appeared on the road before them in plain sight, ready for the taking. They stayed in that place for two days and two nights, feasting and resting. Afterwards, Patrick had a dream. He dreamed that a giant stone fell on him so that he could not move. In the dream, he called upon the prophet Elijah, and then he woke up to rays of sunshine spreading over the horizon. Patrick viewed this dream as a temptation from Satan, and felt that through the sunshine Christ had come to his aid.

By the time the crew reached Italy and sold the dogs, Patrick was ready to leave and make his way back home to Britain, but the voice spoke to him in yet another dream, and told him that he must remain with the ship's crew for two more months. So he did, but when those two months were up he left and made his way northwards to France. By the coast of Provence we find the first real evidence as to where his journeys took him: Lérins Abbey.

Lérins Abbey lay on one of the Lérins Islands in Provence. At the time of Patrick's arrival, it was newly founded. Monasticism was still in its youth, and Lérins was clearly inspired by its Egyptian forerunners. Patrick spent several years with the monks in Lérins and many scholars feel that Patrick's time there was essential to his spiritual growth, and that it was partly responsible for giving Irish Christianity its distinct monastic tendency.

A Missionary's Education

Patrick did eventually make his way back to Britain, where he

traveled to his father's farmstead and was greeted "like a son" by his surviving relatives. Patrick's kin had hoped that he would stay with them, but by the time Patrick finally did reach home the idea of spreading the word of God amongst the Pagans had been growing inside of him.

While home, Patrick had a dream in which a man by the name of Victoricus visited him from Ireland. Victoricus carried a bundle of letters, from which he took one and handed it to Patrick. As Patrick unrolled the scroll and read it, he found that the letter contained voices of the children of Ireland, born and unborn, from the Forest of Fochlad. The voices cried out to him: "We pray you, holy youth, to come and walk amongst us again as you did before." The voices so deeply pierced Patrick's heart that he could not bear to read any more, and so he woke up.

Patrick knew that he could not hope to do much good by simply going to Ireland on his own, a simple Christian peasant with no training and no authority, save for a highly subjective calling. In order to succeed and to make a lasting impact he needed support and resources, to better understand the Christian communities already present in Ireland, and some kind of official sanction.

That is how Patrick ended up going to Autissiodorum, modern Auxerre, in France. It was probably the natural choice for a man hoping to proselytize in Ireland, as Autissiodorum was a popular theological study resort amongst Irish Christians.

It was not long after his arrival in Autissiodorum that the local bishop, Amtor, ordained Patrick a deacon of the church. It was around the same time that two men who would one day come to participate in Patrick's Irish ministries became deacons in Autissiodorum. These men were called Auxilius and Isernius, although Isernius was actually an Irishman who in his native language was called Fith.

People in Autissiodorum were not quite as enthusiastic about Patrick's mission as Patrick was. They even went so far as to encourage him not to go, arguing that he was far too unqualified. Patrick was uneducated, uneloquent, and his Latin was unimpressive. Those kinds of discouraging voices may account for some of the fourteen years it took Patrick to finally go to Ireland.

Although Patrick was not perceived as a scholar, a fact that was often held against him, he must have been quite well read in the Bible — if not when he arrived in Autissiodorum, then at least by the time he had worked in Ireland for some years. Out of the circa 70 books that have at different times been part of the Biblical Canon, Patrick's writings allude to 54. Patrick was also clearly aware of Church history and various contemporary Church developments, referring to at least eight different Church councils, and naming 20 church fathers.

Luckily, not everyone was opposed to Patrick's mission. In his Confessions, Patrick speaks of a friend, although he does not name him, who was sympathetic to Patrick's desire to go to Ireland. Patrick's friend had suggested to him that he needed to be named the Bishop of Ireland in order to succeed. Patrick clearly took the advice to heart.

These were the times of the Pelagian heresy, a belief that human nature was not tainted by original sin and that free will meant that humans could choose between good and evil without the aid or knowledge of God. This heretical belief had gained much ground in Ireland, where the Catholic communities started looking outwards, especially to Britain and France, for help. They wanted a pope. It would have been perfect, if only Pope Celestine I, who had been consulted in the matter, had chosen Patrick for the job. Instead he chose another deacon, Palladius, who was consecrated bishop in 431.

Although we might consider Patrick the natural choice for the job, with the benefit of hindsight, he was actually an unlikely candidate. What Pope Celestine I needed was someone who could take care of the righteous believers in the Christian communities that already existed in Ireland, not someone whose interest lay in converting Pagans. The problem, after all, was not the Pagan neighbors, but the incorrect belief festering within the Christian communities. Palladius was the perfect choice. He had already been involved in quelling the very same heresies in Britain, and he was the man that the Irish themselves wanted for the job.

When it seemed that he had lost his chance at becoming Bishop of Ireland, Patrick stalled no more. He gathered what allies he could find, and within the year he set off for Ireland. He did not get far. Before he even reached the English Channel, the news reached Patrick that Bishop Palladius had died in the north of Ireland.

Where Patrick went from there is uncertain, but we do know that he made a detour. He must either have turned around and returned to Autissiodorum, or, as some scholars believe, continued towards the English Channel to take the boat to Britain.

Theories diverge about what happened next: Patrick was made

Bishop of Ireland. Those that believe that Patrick went to Ireland argue that a new Bishop had to be consecrated by three Bishops at once, which makes Britain a better destination than Autissiodorum. We have no means of knowing if Patrick was sanctioned by the Pope the way that Palladius had been. He did not necessarily have to be. We must understand that the Pope did not have the same role then as he does today. Although the Bishop of Rome had special dispensation to hold a court for clergy, and headed the very important Church at Rome, which was held up as an inspiration to churches everywhere, he was not the leader of Catholic Christianity that he is today.

Regardless, in 432, after fourteen years of waiting, Patrick, Bishop of Ireland, crossed the Irish Sea anew.

First Irish Mission

There is a traditional view of Saint Patrick coming to a wholly Pagan Ireland, turning the island Christian, and driving off the Druids, the upper echelon of Irish Paganism. Magnificent though such a tale is, it may not be fully supported by either the archaeological or the textual evidence. As we have already seen, there was a Bishop of Ireland before Patrick, and he was called to Ireland on behalf of the Irish Christians.

However, this does not devalue Patrick's enormous labor in Ireland, and it most certainly was an enormous labor. In the modern scholar's view, although Patrick did not convert a whole island, he organized the existing Christian communities and brought them into a closer communion with the Church of the Roman empire, and, yes, he also converted a great number of Pagans. This can sound like standard missionary work, but it makes Patrick stand out amongst many other missionary saints stepping into Pagan Europe. Patrick's strong focus on the Roman Empire, its Church and its language sets him apart. Whereas many missionary saints in Patrick's shoes elsewhere attempted to create a national literature, or to slightly change contemporary Christianity either by translating texts into the local language or by rewriting the Gospels in a more local Pagan flavor, Patrick promoted only the Latin language and Latin ways.

The Ireland that Patrick arrived to was not a unified nation. The island was divided into large territories, each one ruled over by large tribal nations made up of smaller communities. Each tribe was ruled by a king or a chieftain, usually elected from one of the noble families of the tribe. The individual tribal territories joined together to create tribal conglomerates, or kingdoms. There were six of them in total in Ireland, each with their own king. Lastly, there was a high king whose power extended across all of Ireland.

Although there were Christian communities in Ireland, they were notoriously difficult to establish due to this tribal system and the high level of social control built into it. Belonging to the tribe was security, and that meant a very high personal loyalty to the tribe and its king or chieftain. A landowner could not simply donate his land for the building of a Church, if it meant displeasing the leader, and, in turn, the tribe. There had to be several layers of consent, which is probably why Patrick so frequently dealt with kings. Even when land was donated, or permission to build a church was given, it was very difficult to establish any form of ecclesiastical center, as Ireland lacked the cities and urban centers of the Roman Empire.

Patrick must have brought with him not only a team of

missionaries, but a large cargo of ecclesiastical items to aid in the conversion of Pagan and creation of churches. According to the Vita sancti Patricii of Tírechán, Patrick brought to Ireland the Gospels, the books of Moses, bells, chalices, altar stones, and patens, the consecrated plates which hold the Eucharist bread. Because Tírechán, unlike his contemporaries describing similar missions elsewhere, put no effort into describing the glory or luxury of these objects, it is generally thought that in this case, like in so many others, Patrick's mission was quite austere. In the Metrical Life of Saint Patrick we learn just how austere Patrick's mission was:

> "Then he slept on a cold bed of stone,
> And with a wet cover was dressed;
> A stone was his pillow each night —
> Such was the saint's nightly rest."

Saint Sechnall's Hymn of Saint Patrick, which was probably written during Patrick's lifetime, tells us this of Patrick's mission in Ireland:

> "He was sent by God to fish with the nets of faith,
> and thus draw the believers of the world unto
> grace. The chosen Gospel talents of Christ were
> dispensed by him with usury amongst the Irish

people. He preached by works as well as by words, and stimulated to holiness by his example. He was humble in spirit and by body, and in his flesh bore the stigmata of Christ, in whose cross alone he glorified, being sustained by its saving power."

Tradition has it that the island plain of Dalriada in Northern Ireland is where Patrick began his mission. Patrick, it is said, chose to start there because he wanted to persuade his former slave master to become a Christian.

According to the legends, his master refused to submit despite bribes of gold, because it would be unseemly to become a subject to his former slave. However, as we have already seen, Patrick himself claims that he did not serve under a master in the north, but in the west. Nonetheless, there is much textual evidence that Patrick did spend much time in the north of Ireland, and he also spent time in Connaught, where he himself claims that his former master lived. It is almost impossible to get a clear picture of precisely how Patrick moved across the island, so our account of his first mission in Ireland is by necessity a rough sketch, sometimes internally chronological,

The legends of Patrick, found in several sources including the Vita tripartita Sancti Patricii, tell us that Patrick spent his first

Easter as Bishop of Ireland on top of the hill of Slane, in Meath. On Easter Eve, Patrick and his friends lit the paschal fire. Most likely, they had chosen that place because they knew that it was within sight, albeit miles away from, the hill of Tara, the seat of the high king of Ireland, and on this very night the high king had gathered kings and nobles to a very solemn feast at his palace.

It was a custom, at such a solemn festival, that no fire may be lit until the king had lit his at Tara. Patrick's paschal fire obviously contradicted this very rule, and as the fire roared on the hill of Slane it could be seen at Tara from across the vast plain. The high king Laoghaire consulted his druids, and they said: "O King, unless this fire that you see is quenched this very night, it will never be quenched. And all those who kindled it will overcome us all and seduce all of the people of your realm."

Laoghaire then ordered to have nine chariots prepared, and with a party that included the queen and Laoghaire's two head druids, Lochru and Lucetmael, he drove across the plain to the hill of Slane. As the chariots came to a halt, Patrick came down the hill to meet them. He fell into a heated debate with the druids, Lochru and Lucetmael, about divinity and the ways of the world.

Lochru lost his temper and uttered some very harsh words against the Christian faith. That was more than Patrick was willing to take. He looked into the eyes of Lochru, and he prayed to God that the blasphemer be flung into the air and dashed into the ground. Immediately, Lochru was thrown into the air and dashed against the ground so that his head was smashed into hundreds of little pieces. Enraged, king Laoghaire ordered his men to seize Patrick, but the saint said: "Let God arise, and let his enemies be scattered!" Darkness fell on the plain and the earth quaked so that the king's soldiers fell upon each other instead of Patrick, and only king Laoghaid, his queen and Lucetmael survived.

The following day, king Laoghaid was once again feasting with the Irish nobles at his palace at Tara. Suddenly, Patrick and his companions appeared amongst them, even though the door had been locked, to speak to them again about Christianity. The druid Lucetmael offered Patrick a cup of ale, but Patrick had a sneaking suspicion that something was not quite right.

He blessed the cup and all of the ale turned to ice. Patrick turned the cup upside down, and out of the cup dropped a single drop of poison. When Patrick turned the cup upright again and blessed it once more, the ale became liquid again and he could drink it without suffering harm.

Lucetmael then challenged Patrick. "Let us work miracles on the plain," he said. "Let us bring down snow on the land." "I will not bring down anything against the will of God," Patrick replied, but Lucetmael persisted and brought down waist-high snow with his incantations.

"Now remove it," said Patrick. "I cannot," was the druid's response, "until the same time tomorrow."

"You can do evil, but not good," said Patrick, and he blessed the plain and all of the snow disappeared.

Next, the druid brought darkness upon the plain, but like the snow he could not dissipate it. Patrick, however, could. Then, they built a hut. Half of it was built from green wood and half of it from dry wood. Patrick's companion, Benignus, was made to wear the druid's cloak and the druid was made to wear Patrick's. Benignus sat in the dry part of the hut, and the druid sat in the green part. Then, they set fire to the hut. Patrick prayed over Benignus, who came out unharmed from the rubble even though the druid's cloak had burned to pieces around him, but the fire consumed Lucetmael, while Patrick's coat was left unscathed.

After seeing Patrick's great power through God, Laoghaire agreed to protect Patrick within his realm. Although Laoghaire himself was not persuaded to convert, his brother Conall was.

Conall, having undergone his baptism, gave Patrick some land to build a church near his own house, at the site of modern Donagh-Patrick. Patrick did not have the same luck with all of Laoghaire's brothers, though. His brother Coirpre attempted to have Patrick murdered, but when Coirpre could not buy off Patrick's servants and have them give up their master he punished them instead. At the hill of Uisneach in southern Meath, Coirpre's son also attempted to murder Patrick, but he only succeeded in murdering some of Patrick's traveling companions. After this, Patrick visited the sacred standing stone of Coithrige and inscribed on it his name and a cross. Patrick then cursed both Coirpre and his son so that their line would never be the high king of Ireland.

Having established several churches in Meath, Patrick headed westwards to Connaught, where legends tell us there was a famous Pagan idol out of stone, covered with gold and silver, inside a circle of twelve sacred pillar-stones. Crom Cruaich, it was called, and the legends say that it was commonly worshiped in Ireland as well as in Britain.

The legend goes that Patrick went up to the idol and struck it down with his staff. However, some scholars feel that this story raises a number of questions. If it was indeed a site of national and international cultic importance, it seems unlikely that

Patrick could have done any of this without the backing of local kings or even the high king. Given how small significance the event has been given in the Patrick cycle it's unlikely that, if it happened, it really was such a great and widely worshiped deity.

Patrick journeyed far and wide in that first decade in Ireland. He even traveled to the northern islands. According to the later legends he also communicated directly with the Lord in those days, not merely receiving dreams as before. One story goes that Patrick and his companions went to visit an island. There, Patrick saw a withered old woman in front of a house, and he asked: "Whence is the hag?" "Great is her infirmity," answered a young man. "She is a descendant of mine," he continued. "If you could see the mother of this girl, o cleric, she is more infirm still." Puzzled, Patrick asked how the young man's descendants had come to look so much older than him. "We are here since the time of Christ," the young man responded. "He came to visit us when He was on earth amongst men, and we made a feast for him, and he blessed our house and blessed ourselves. But his blessing reached not our children, and we shall be here without age or decay for ever."

He continued: "And it is long since thy coming was foretold to us, and God prophesied to us that thou wouldst come to preach to the Gaels; and he left a token with us, his crosier, to be given to thee." "I will not take it," Patrick said, "until He himself gives me His crosier."

Patrick remained three days and three nights with the island people, after which he went to a mountain called Hermon, where the Lord appeared to him. The Lord commanded Patrick to go and preach to the Gaels, and "Patrick brought three requests of him — (1) to be His right hand in the Kingdom of Heaven; (2) that Patrick might be the judge of the Gaels on the Day of Judgment; (3) as much as the nine companions could carry of gold and silver to give to the Gaels for believing."

Second Irish Mission

For a decade Patrick wandered Ireland, converting Pagans
and organizing the Christian communities. Then, some time
around the year 441-443, when Patrick must have been around
50-55 years old he went to Rome. According to the Vita sancti
Patricii of Muirchu moccu Machtheni, Patrick set off for Rome,
but on his way there he stopped in Autissiodorum, where he had
hoped to get some further training for his Ireland mission.

Patrick no doubt saw the church at Rome as a superior model
Church, and like so many others in his age he wanted to see it
with his own eyes. Patrick's visit to Rome may have involved
receiving some practical advice from Pope Leo the Great, such as
the Pope gave Saint Augustine of Canterbury for his mission
amongst the Anglo-Saxons. Patrick may also have hoped to
acquire some relics for Ireland such important relics as remains
of Saint Peter and Saint Paul were housed in Rome and bishops
from all over the west were hoping for shares in the remains.

When Patrick returned to Ireland what was probably the most
decisive act of his entire mission occurred: the establishment of
the monastery of Ardd Mache, Ireland's greatest ecclesiastical
center. This monastery lay in the kingdom of Oriel, which was
either entirely or at least in part ruled by a king by the name of

Daire. Although king Daire was not a Christian himself, he was not hostile towards Christianity. When Patrick requested the land on top of Ardd Mache, the hill of Macha, named after the semi-divine or divine mythical Pagan queen Macha, Daire did not give him the summit, but could be persuaded to allow Patrick to build a monastery at the bottom of the hill.

Those were the earliest beginnings of the chief ecclesiastical city in Ireland. A circular space was marked out, 140 ft in diameter. Within this circle, Patrick and his companions erected a wooden structure for the monks, with a small oratory and a kitchen.

Winning king Daire over entirely, however, was no easy feat. There were initially some frictions. King Daire's squire once drove the king's horse onto the monastery grounds, although Patrick had told him not to. The next day the horse was dead, and the squire went to the king and told him that the Christians had killed it. Outraged, Daire ordered that Patrick be killed. Immediately, Daire fell ill, and his wife said: "It must be the Christian who made this happen. Someone must go quickly and let his blessing be brought to us, and then my husband will be well. Tell those who went to slay him to stop!" Patrick gave the king's emissaries some consecrated water, which they first sprinkled on the dead horse so that it came back alive, and then it was used to heal king Daire.

King Daire went to the monastery to pay respect to Patrick and to give him a large imported bronze vessel. In Pagan Ireland, the giving and receiving of gifts was very important and the king was rather disappointed with Patrick's response to his fine gift. Instead of a grand response to the grand gesture, Patrick simply appeared to say "gratzicum," complete gibberish. In reality, it was the Latin phrase for "thank you," "gratias agamus," that Patrick had uttered but the Pagan Irish king did not speak sufficient Latin to know this. Angry over the perceived slight, king Daire sent his servants to fetch the vessel back from Patrick, and when they returned he inquired as to what the bishop had said. "He said gratzicum," they told the king. Daire responded: "What? Gratzicum when it was given and gratzicum when it was taken away! It is a firm word, and for his gratzicum he shall have his cauldron." So, king Daire went himself to Patrick and said: "Keep the cauldron, for you are a steadfast and unchangeable man." And for his perceived strength, Patrick was given the superior land on top of Ardd Mache.

Throughout his years on Ireland, a large part of Patrick's work was about laying down rules for the clergy and for practitioners. For the most part this organizing seems to have been done not as a part of a greater ideal so much as a response to arising questions and problems. Of special interest is Patrick's ordination that no cleric from Britain could minister in Ireland, unless he had a letter from his superior. It was also decided that all Irish clergy, even priests, were to be tonsured, and their wives had to be veiled, nor were a monk and nun to ride in the same carriage. It was also made prohibited to accept alms from Pagans.

Another significant aspect of his work was the creation of churches and the consecration of clergy. There are many churches named in the literature that have been established by Saint Patrick or by one of his disciples, but for the most part they are only names to us. Their location cannot be known with any degree of certainty. Nor can scholars agree on exactly how many bishops Patrick consecrated in his time on Ireland. Some say that he consecrated as many as 450, others claim that he consecrated as few as 150 bishops. Others still argue that the legends about the consecration of bishops must all be false since consecration legally required the presence of three bishops, and Patrick was at the beginning the only bishop in Ireland. In addition to these clergymen, Patrick himself claimed to have baptized thousands.

He prided himself especially on converting the daughters of kings into virgins of Christ, and since these maidens often took the vows against their fathers' wills, for these young women converting generally lead to persecution from their parents.

Patrick also performed many miracles in those days. Amongst other things, he fed fourteen thousand men with only five cows, and revived dozens of people from death, even people who had been buried for many years. He also famously banished all snakes from Ireland, chasing them into the sea after a 40 day long fast.

One of the important duties of Irish Christians under the leadership of Patrick was the redemption of Christian captives from slavery. This is also the topic of a text that Patrick wrote towards the end of his life, the Epistle to Coroticus.

Coroticus was a powerful chieftain of sorts ruling the Strathclyde area in western Scotland. His seat was at the Rock of Clyde, now modern Dumbarton, where the Vita tripartita Sancti Patricii claims that Patrick was born. A significant part of Coroticus's revenue came from plundering neighbors, at which point slaves were taken. The same was true of the heathen Picts, Coroticus's allies living in the north east of Ireland and north of Scotland. One such raiding event in particular outraged Patrick, when the Picts fell upon one of Patrick's Irish communities and killed and enslaved neophyte Christians, still dressed in white for their baptismal ceremony. If Patrick was not at the ceremony in person, he was certainly nearby, for the very next day he sent his emissaries to Coroticus, whom he held responsible, to demand the release of captives and the return of treasures. Coroticus and his soldiers were Romans, and Christians themselves, so they did not feel particularly responsible for what the Picts did. Instead of helping Patrick, they mocked his request.

In response, Patrick wrote a strong letter to the general Christian community of Strathclyde, hoping to turn the public opinion against Coroticus in order to make him act differently. The tyrant and his soldiers, Patrick told his Christian countrymen, were not to be shown respect, or dealt with at all.

Sometime after writing the Epistle to Coroticus, Patrick wrote his Confessions. He was by then an old man and was nearing the end of his life.

There is some argument about how and when Saint Patrick eventually died. Tradition has it that it occurred on March 17, hence the celebration of Saint Patrick's Day on that date. The traditional year is 493, at which time Patrick would have been around 105 years old. The proposed dates range from the year 420 to 493, with most people believing he died at earliest in the year 460, around the age of 77. How he died is unfortunately just as uncertain and the date. Given Patrick's age, we may assume that he died peacefully from old age. Like most early saints, the

Catholic Church never canonized Saint Patrick.

The quest for Saint Patrick provides a picture of two Saint Patricks. The Patrick of his own writings, and of the very earliest texts, is a very humble man, if slightly bitter about the resistance he has met from his fellow Christians outside of Ireland, and he is extremely aware of his very earthly limitations. He is an organizer, a writer of letters, and a perpetual, if not always a great, student, as well as a teacher. He quotes frequently from the Bible, and he works tirelessly to build community and provide for Irish Christians a place in the Roman Empire. He is a teenage sinner, turned convert, turned Bishop, and a lesser nobleman, turned slave, turned clergyman.

On the other side stands the Patrick of miraculous tales, whose childhood deeds echo the medieval tales of the childhood deeds of Jesus Christ himself. Everything he touches is blessed, and he is so sure in his own status as chosen by God that when he speaks to the Lord he does not hesitate to make demands for himself, such as arranging special powers for himself in Heaven, and demanding worldly goods.

The seeker who wishes to compromise and merge both images into one may choose to scale back some of the more fantastical elements of Patrick's many miracles and read between the lines.

In that case, we see a Patrick who does not compromise his faith and is not afraid of antagonizing kings, a Patrick who is fearless in the face of danger, and a Patrick who at great risk always has the interest of the Irish Christians at heart. At the end of the day, we cannot know for certain which image of Patrick is historically accurate, but the journey has hopefully brought us closer to the wonderful saint.

Prayers of Saint Patrick

Prayers for the Faithful

May the Strength of God guide us.

May the Power of God preserve us.
May the Wisdom of God instruct us.
May the Hand of God protect us.
May the Way of God direct us.
May the Shield of God defend us.
May the Angels of God guard us.
- Against the snares of the evil one.

May Christ be with us!
May Christ be before us!
May Christ be in us,
Christ be over all!

May Thy Grace, Lord,
Always be ours,
This day, O Lord, and forevermore. Amen.

Prayer for God's Protection and Christ's Presence

As I arise today, may the strength of God pilot me, the power of God uphold me, the wisdom of God guide me. May the eye of God look before me, the ear of God hear me, the word of God speak for me. May the hand of God protect me, the way of God lie before me, the shield of God defend me, the host of God save me. May Christ shield me today...Christ with me, Christ before me, Christ behind me, Christ in me, Christ beneath me, Christ above me, Christ on my right, Christ on my left, Christ when I lie down, Christ when I sit, Christ when I stand, Christ in the heart of everyone who thinks of me, Christ in the mouth of everyone who speaks of me, Christ in every eye that sees me, Christ in every ear that hears me. Amen.

Lorica of Saint Patrick

I arise today

Through a mighty strength, the invocation of the Trinity,
Through a belief in the Threeness,
Through confession of the Oneness
Of the Creator of creation.

I arise today
Through the strength of Christ's birth and His baptism,
Through the strength of His crucifixion and His burial,
Through the strength of His resurrection and His ascension,
Through the strength of His descent for the judgment of doom.

I arise today
Through the strength of the love of cherubim,
In obedience of angels,
In service of archangels,
In the hope of resurrection to meet with reward,
In the prayers of patriarchs,
In preachings of the apostles,
In faiths of confessors,
In innocence of virgins,
In deeds of righteous men.

I arise today
Through the strength of heaven;
Light of the sun,
Splendor of fire,
Speed of lightning,
Swiftness of the wind,
Depth of the sea,
Stability of the earth,
Firmness of the rock.

I arise today
Through God's strength to pilot me;
God's might to uphold me,

God's wisdom to guide me,
God's eye to look before me,
God's ear to hear me,
God's word to speak for me,
God's hand to guard me,
God's way to lie before me,
God's shield to protect me,
God's hosts to save me
From snares of the devil,
From temptations of vices,
From every one who desires me ill,
Afar and anear,
Alone or in a mulitude.

I summon today all these powers between me and evil,
Against every cruel merciless power that opposes my body and
soul,
Against incantations of false prophets,
Against black laws of pagandom,
Against false laws of heretics,
Against craft of idolatry,
Against spells of women and smiths and wizards,
Against every knowledge that corrupts man's body and soul.
Christ shield me today
Against poison, against burning,
Against drowning, against wounding,
So that reward may come to me in abundance.

Christ with me, Christ before me, Christ behind me,
Christ in me, Christ beneath me, Christ above me,
Christ on my right, Christ on my left,
Christ when I lie down, Christ when I sit down,
Christ in the heart of every man who thinks of me,
Christ in the mouth of every man who speaks of me,
Christ in the eye that sees me,
Christ in the ear that hears me.

I arise today

Through a mighty strength, the invocation of the Trinity,
Through a belief in the Threeness,
Through a confession of the Oneness
Of the Creator of creation